Collages

by Michelle Gunner

Published by New Generation Publishing in 2020

First Edition

ISBN

Paperback	978-1-80031-417-7
Hardback	978-1-80031-416-0

www.newgeneration-publishing.com

New Generation Publishing

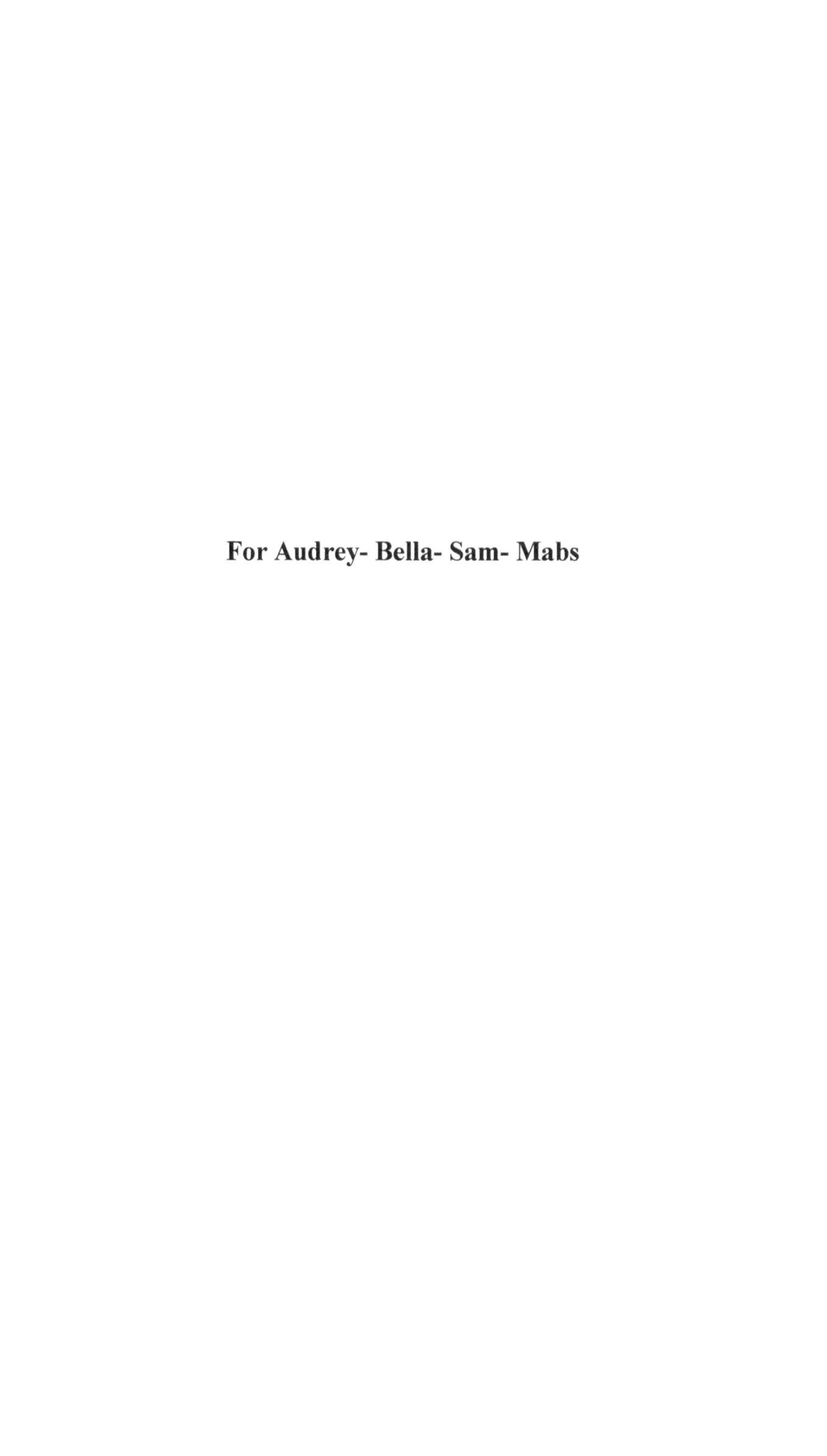

For Audrey- Bella- Sam- Mabs

Acknowledgements

I would like to thank Jan Moran Neil, Metroland Workshop and Gerard Benson, friends and mentors for their help and encouragement.

Acknowledgements are also due to the editors of the following publications in which some of these poems first appeared:

First Time
Leaves of Metroland
Lines of Metroland
Rhyme & Reason
South

Publications

'Esmeralda' commended in The Chiltern Writers Group in Creative Writing

'The Intruder' commended finalist in the Chiltern Writers Poetry Competition

'Queen of Hearts' in First time anthology

'Perfidious Albion' in South Magazine

'Esmeralda' Poem of the week in the Bucks Free Press

Also highly commended for Save the Heroes competition for her novel an ***An Orchid in Winter***

CONTENTS

THE BASQUE COUNTRY

Vive la Liberté

Across the Pyrenees' misty summits
vultures circled,
the mirage of freedom flickered.
When Jean said,
"You are safe now,"
hope returned in the stranger's eyes.
Agile as a deer Jean made a quick descent
back to his sullied land, reaching the shelter
before fat warm drops, twined into torrential rain,
and grumbles of thunder turned into a roar,
echoing, booming, rolling around the mountains
into the plain.
Manic blue flashes danced
in and out of billowing trees.

These will never belong to the enemy.

When the storm was spent
he resumed his walk through the soaking ferns,
his two boys and gentle wife
would be waiting for his return,
and from his bag he would magic
a handful of cherries, wild mushrooms,
chestnuts bursting out of goose pimpled skins.
There would always be flowers for her;
lilies of the valley or wild orchids in the spring,
forget-me-nots and daisies in the summer,
autumn crocuses and blue gentians,
winter fallen stars: velvety Edelweiss.

These will never belong to the enemy.

At the clearing a sound startled him.
It was not the hedgehog shuffling
through autumn leaves
or a rabbit caught in a snare.
“Halt.”
Defiant he walked on...
The bullet reached its target.
He stumbled, fell...
taking away a handful of grass.
The pungent smell of humid earth,
the familiar owl's cry
and the ever spinning sky,

These will always belong to him.

Post War Inventory

Retour à la Villa La Nive

In our drawers
their knives and forks in a row
and in our cupboard
their white porcelain plates,
'Made in Germany.'

In the attic, my doll
head cracked
hair shorn
limbs shattered
clothes torn.

I just want to remember
the exuberant mornings
when swifts called,
drowsy afternoons
when floorboards creaked
and doors whispered, long evenings
when in my father's arms
I watched the sun bounce
from mountain to mountain.

The Bond

My grandmothers rarely met -
the villa being quite a way
from the farmhouse.

Besides, they spoke a different language:
my Parisian grandmother
tall, hair à la Marlene Dietrich
talked paintings, theatre, music...
My Basque grandmother,
small, high voltage temper
to match electric eyes,
talked harvest, pigs, chickens...

But when they met
they sat in the kitchen and talked of our prowess
and the scent of Chanel Number Five
mingled with the smell of cabbage soup.

The Knife

My father's Opinel with its stubby handle
and cut throat blade
was a blot on the icy landscape
of dazzling white, silver and crystal,
napkins so stiff they could not absorb stains.

It was a wound to his mother's pride,
the symbol of his rebellion:
his refusal to dress up for dinner,
his familiarity with servants
and later on, his marrying below his station.

In this modest household,
his knife was needed, admired, loved.
"Only John's can carve through that tough meat!"

Many years on, servants, crystal and silver gone
I still hear my grandmother sigh, "John must you?"
When, as we sat down to meals,
he would extricate his knife from his pocket
and lay it beside his plate.

I have it now. The handle warm to my touch,
The blade rusty and uneven.
I found it in a box with sepia photographs
of mother holding son and a bundle of her letters
tied up with blue ribbon.

For all my father's endeavours
he could not sever the umbilical cord.

Children at Play

They call
as you slide into clouds and sky
conjured in a pool of rain.

They scorn
at your grazed knees and skirt torn
conquering trees in the garden.

They force
leaden mixtures when you are sated
with nectar and ambrosia.

You sometimes glance
at their worlds
and are surprised at their lives, their tears.

Bewitched

"I am lost," cries the frightened child.
I have left my garden this morning
deaf to Mother's warnings.
I have crossed over the bridge and followed the river;
here, a joyful cascade, there a shimmering mirror.

Now night has fallen and I am in a strange place.
No stars dance in the opaque sky,
all birds' songs have ceased.
The forest is filled with curdling screams.
Trees are giants waiting to engulf me.
Wherever I turn, thorns
like cats' claws spring from nowhere,
scratching and wounding.
I stand, petrified
and I long to be in Mother's arms
in our scented garden.

La Bidaossa

In a dark pool of the river
a trout was feeding.
Sweeping down, branches caressed the stream
making the task of the quiet angler difficult.
A soft south wind rippled the water and
disturbed the weeping willows.
My uncle recalled:
"I was your age when over this rickety bridge
I saw young men running from Franco's bayonets.
Some no more than boys.
Only a handful made it across."

It was then that I saw the river change colour.

Pie in the Sky – Les Palombes

"Succulent!" said the stranger
at the restaurant, by the river
in Bidarray.

During the long winters months
hunters had repaired nets
that now web the French Pyrenees.
Palombes are leaving their frozen shores
For the autumn mountains.

Across the cobalt blue sky
a wave of palombes mask the sun.
To foil the claws of birds of prey,
they spin and whirl –a circus act
and dive down into the nets.
(Alas not there to save lives.)
Thus beaks, wings feathers,
become entangled into the mesh.
Few escape and make their way to Spain
up and up over the reddening mountains.
While the others…

"Succulent," said the stranger
in the restaurant in Bidarray.

Moody

Clouds in the sky and in my mind.
Silver stars in midnight blue
and in my heart.

Along, along the wind
blows on my mood,
one morning blue, afternoon smile.

What am I?
Sad, happy?
For ever changing.

Along, along
the wind blows on my mood
like the clouds in the sky.

Harvesting Memories

From the attic window of the villa 'La Nive' I watched
'La Montagne des Dames' exhibit a new robe for each
season.

We ran into the autumn wind, propelled like leaves,
we gathered chestnuts to crackle on the open fire,
we climbed trees to gorge on juicy purple figs...
Sometimes the river would burst its banks, storms
menaced.
My brother and I took refuge under blankets.

Winter drew magic patterns on our window panes.
Multi-coloured candles adorned our Christmas tree.
Later, stripped of all its finery, hissing and spitting
it blazed in the chimney.
We watched shadows dance on the walls,
soothed by Mother's gentle voice reading fairy stories.

Mother's white camellia never survived the spring.
Frost left rusty marks on the petals.
"Look, Maman. The pink camellia has bloomed!"
But we couldn't take away the sadness in her eyes.
Years later I did see it flower-
a pearly lustre against a blue sky.
By then she was not there to see it.
In the summer, a canopy of wisteria draped the porch,
and fat pompoms of hydrangeas guarded the villa.
Morning cries of swifts promised a picnic.
In his shiny canoe, Father braved cascades.
We frolicked in rock pools
under the melancholy gaze of Mother
until we heard, high above us, the six o'clock train
which had meandered through Bayonne,Bidarray
and St Jean Pied de Port -
and knew that it was time to climb up the steep path

between overgrown hedgerows, stinging nettles,
and thorns of wild roses which perfumed our summers.
Mostly I ended up asleep in my father's arms
wondering on waking, how I got to my bed.

But the autumn wind blew again,
scattering each one of us to all corners of the world
and far beyond.

PARIS

Stuffed Museum

My grandfather – a gentleman
(lover of England), all tweeds and golf trousers,
metallic frames encircling myopic eyes,
took on the hefty task of educating
my uncultured mind and Thursdays
were Museum days.

In the dusty corridors of the Louvre
my grandfather tried to stimulate my interest
"It is extraordinary how the jocund eyes
follow you wherever you are!
And that smile is truly impenetrable."
"Absolutely riveting!"

"Look at the Venus de Milo
don't you find her shape remarkable?"
"*Yes, beautiful.*"

But then I thought. Where are her arms?
I much prefer David
Even if it's small he's got it all
Isn't time we went?

"Tea time. Let's go to the patisserie,"
said Grandfather on cue.

Now I call this art, the red and bright
strawberry tarts, the yellow plums,
the colours are just divine.
I am mummified by all the choice

"Next week we'll see the sarcophagus."
Thank God for the strawberry tarts!

In The Park Monceau- The Last of the Camondo*

Swings fly up to sky
skipping ropes whip ground,
blue, red, yellow balloons drift away
far far away.
Little girl in candy- striped dress cries.

Under a weeping willow
jeunes filles en fleur tease boys;
boys who try stealing kisses
from dewy skin.

Hidden from children at play,
up some mossy stairs
in a sleepy palace an old man waits;
waits for his son, daughter, grandchildren
in vain.

It's winter now and the park is deserted
Where is the girl in candy striped dress?
Jeunes filles en fleurs, and amorous boys?
Drifted and lost in time.

Depleted hedge no longer hides the mansion
-spectre from the past emerging from the mist.
Where is the old man's son? Gone to war...
Where are the daughters and grandchildren?
Deported everyone.

* *With no heir, Moise de Camondo left his treasures to the nation . A nation which had let him down*

Divertissement

We were the darlings of the Opera de Paris
my brother and I. How we danced, it was bliss!
I was a feather, floating on the stage,
he had an impressive ribcage.
Sergei Lifar (impresario between Diaghilev and Nureyev)
had a *penchant* for my brother's *Arabesques*,
I could tell by the way he yelled brrrravo! Brrravo! –
He was Russian you know – (defected)
when he (my brother) danced the elf
in a ballet by Prokofiev, from a story by Turgenev.
He (Sergei) ignored my display of *Pirouettes*.
It wasn't all castanets and *minuets*,
my brother dropped me after I leapt in the air,
I broke a leg as I fell.
He said a swan in the wings got him distracted.
He had to dance, the Nutcracker solo. How unfair!
The audience didn't like his *entrechats*. It was a shame but
our *Pas de Deux* was never the same...
I think he envied my tutu collection,
I found him trying on my favourite pink one.
I don't see much of him now, he tours the country with
Sergei
while I flutter my duster around the house
like a sugar plump fairy.

Esmeralda*

After the ball, senses jaded,
they return to their gilded palace.
And when the blackamoor, in his midnight costume,
snuffs out the last candle,
princes and princesses, dukes and duchesses,
sink into baldachin beds.
Under goose-feathered eiderdowns,
they sleep, undisturbed...

In a courtyard of Notre Dame,
beggars have gathered.
When Esmeralda sings,
her sweet voice bringing hope, they sing.
When Esmeralda dances, swaying her curves,
to the jingle of her tambourine, they dance.
Esmeralda is their Queen.

From dawn, beggars wait
for grandees to promenade
their powdered edifice of curls and lice,
their brocades and rotting silks.
Beggars wait for their majesties to meander
from Tuileries to Place de La Bastille.
Beggars wait for largesse...They wait and wait...

But tonight, Esmeralda will sing and dance.
Tonight, Esmeralda will be their queen.

*Esmeralda. Heroine of *The Hunchback of Notre Dame* by V. Hugo

Madame Spirgelle

Madame Spirgelle rented a room
in our flat Rue de Courcelles.
With a gamine haircut and black-rimmed eyes
she looked a little *louche* and had an air of a fallen angel,
Madame Spirgelle.
We often visited her *boudoir le soir.*
Guerlain perfume and Gauloises fumes
sent our heads in a spin
I often sat at her dressing tables and marvelled
at jewellery of fake gold and silver.
My brother was partial to her dresses *en dentelles*,
cobweb-like marvels.

One day we found a tearful Madame Spirgelle:
'"*You must go.*" "Grandmother had said.
"You are a bad influence on these innocent children."
As the lift spirited her from our lives, we cried.
At dinner my grandfather looked strained
and forlorn. But a conclusion was drawn,
we were never to speak of Madame Spirgelle ever again.

Objets Perdus, Objets Trouvés

In an antique shop, Boulevard St. Germain,
among an array of statues,
clocks, dolls, mirrors, chandeliers
my grandfather's lost painting!

In our flat on Quai d'Anjou,
I had watched the Seine flowing
from his brush: sky smudged
pearly grey, dipping into the river
and touches of green
on the mourning suits of trees
to create the coming spring.

The dealer praises the delicacy of hues
but he cannot see
beyond this early spring scene;
a child observing the painter,
her brother practising the piano,
their grandmother playing endless patience
and a vase of anemones on damascene.

Still Life: Anemones

I often glance at the anemones,
their mauves and pinks as vibrant
as the day Grandfather and I bought them
from the market Rue Bayen.

While Grandmother prayed for our souls,
he and I fought our way to crowded stalls,
buying oysters – a Sunday treat,
then sniffing Camembert
for one on the right side of ripe,
probing hearts of lettuces, caressing oranges
and always we bought anemones!
Later, in the dented silver vase
their gypsy corollas were on parade,
beside goblets, oysters' shells sucked dry,
a chicken carcass, salad leaves in a pool of oil
and the remains of an apple tart.

Cigarette smoke ribboned the air,
wrapped itself around my brother's head,
and our giggles mingled with
the adults' droning voices.

The anemones were doubly useful:
to please Grandmother who missed her garden
and to be painted by Grandfather
all through a lazy afternoon.

Painting Juliette

Buried in the big armchair I watch.
Her student clothes discarded
she steps from behind the screen
majestic in her bearing,
hair swept up, vermilion on her lips-
an exotic queen.

The fringes of a shawl
play Hide and Seek
with her shimmering body,
cascade between the deep valley
of her uncovered breasts
and shadow a mysterious triangle.

She abandons herself to the green sofa,
stretches, shawl about to slip from amber shoulders,
and I wait...
“It's time for your homework,” says Grandfather,
thumb a distance from his eye.

Later, bathed in the cold light of the bathroom
the mirror reflects my image:
all ribcage and flatness.
How I envied Juliette.

She looks at me now, same smile,
all mysteries unveiled...
but somehow, she looks slimmer.

In Drawing Her Portrait

She turns her face towards him.
How long since he looked into her eyes?
Those eyes – once he had lost himself
in their infinite blue.

They had watched over a child,
and dimmed with its last breath,
those eyes sunk in shadows
as if forever in mourning.

Her tears became ice,
love froze in their hearts.
She found refuge in God, he, elsewhere.

His crayon outlines her mouth like a caress.
That mouth he had kissed with such thirst,
became sadder with each of his infidelities.

Now he observes the finished portrait.
Her eyes are softer, there's
a faint smile starting on her lips.

A faint smile is starting on her lips.

The Annunciation

In the studio

"Come on Mary, love, look more virginal.
Gabriel don't be such a wimp, perk up that wing,
it's gone all limp! Oh God! That dove is ridiculously
small and who has put the lilies in that bowl?
Freeze. At last we have a wrap."

In the Museum

There is a commotion,
the speaker for animal rights wants a fight;
"Hundreds of beetles were crushed for the colour of that
wall.
I call that cruelty to animals, down with that altar piece."
"I beg your pardon," exclaimed the Afghan ambassador.
"They raided all the Lapis Lazuli from our mines,
to create the azure of that sky.
This masterpiece must be mine."

"Hang on," cries the angry rabbi.
'They've nicked all our coins
to gild those blessed Auras.
I declare that's our Maestá."

Meanwhile the angel Gabriel
is still breaking the bad news to Mary.

**The Annunciation* is a fragment of the *Maestá* and is currently on display at the National Gallery and the other bits around the world.

Dear Picasso

What have we done Pablo
to make you hate us so?
Your view of the female form
is so far from the norm:
eye on forehead
and a big 'derriere',
nose, lips, ears askew
your drawing of our anatomy
makes me blue.
They say you paint all day
and all night you screw.
Forgive my worry
but don't you come unstuck
when you fuck?
And for god sake
how can you, without mistake
know which end to take?

A Parrot is Perched on Salvador Dali's Moustache

A woman at the exhibition thinks-
This is no place for a parrot!
The parrot who can read into people's minds says,
I have as much right to be here as you.
Besides you silly moo who else has the chance to view the world from the master's moustache?
What a rude bird...Quel dommage,
he has such a divine plumage!
I wonder if he dyes his feathers?
I am not as vain as you.
Can't I talk to myself
without your interference?
Please yourself, antisocial personage!

A man passing by is struck by the beauteous parrot,
pretty Polly, prrretty Polly.
The parrot's beak stays firmly closed.
What a hopeless parrot, he can't even speak.
What a fool, calling me Polly! Do I call him Mrs Smith?

Dancing Among the Constellations

Clouds and rainbows for costumes,
I watch the dancers go
pirouetting around our planet
along the stars and the sun.
Earthbound no more, flying,
propelled to the moon
leaping to undreamt heights.
Feet darting between Jupiter and Saturn,
arabesques stretching into infinity.
Feathers scattered in the universe
they dance, dance ecstatic,
an extravagant, extra-terrestrial ballet
In the Silence of Eternity.

ENGLAND

Perfidious Albion
or How to Keep your Daughters at Home

"Must you go to England? Such a strange nation,"
they cried in unison.
"Full of English, a funny breed
unable to properly feed.
Open them up, what do you see?
Thousands of cups of tea
floating in their tummies." *
"Remember at Waterloo, Trafalgar and Agincourt
their behaviour was very poor," Father said.
"The sun does not suit their complexions and women
only look smart in tweeds and macs," Mother said.
"Zey boil zeir beefe," Granmama said with grief.
"They burnt Joan of Arc at the stake
and have not paid enough for that mistake,"said Papa.
"Zey also burn zeir steak, pouah!
Have you seen zeir petit pois?" echoed Granmama.
"At least your virtue will be safe," they mused blissfully,
"The British are the only nation
which think of duty at the height of passion
and to undress causes them so much distress."
"Oh," said I sadly. "I might not go to England.
What about Spain?"

"Well Franco he was a so and so.
Women wear a silly mantilla
and the nation eat a strange concoction called Paella...etc...

* Les Carnets du Major Thompson by Pierre Daninos

If Only English Was More Like French...

Misunderstanding.

The English language has no other to compare
said our great Monsieur Flaubert.
It's so full of subtlety
that an Englishman never appears to be nasty.
If he asks you whether you have any family left,
it is not because he thinks you are bereft,
but he wants to know if you are
as old as he thinks you are!
If you are boring him, he will say,
in the most delightful way
I shan't detain you any longer.
-a little more refined than, *I am out of here!*
(which our American cousins would prefer).
If you should hear
Don't ring me. I'll ring you, I fear
that his ill-concealed aim
is never to see you again.
Full of good intentions he'll chime
Come to dinner sometime...
But you might die of malnutrition
waiting for that invitation.
It would take me more than one reincarnation
to comprehend the innuendo
of that perfect lingo...
If I asked you to express your thoughts on this poem,
I can now hear you exclaim
Excellent idea but why don't you try to write it again -
in French...

The Work Chop

"Ummm..mn..mm"
Pregnant Pause.
……………………

"Strong Poem."
More pause.

……………………
"Difficult subject"
"It's a fact."
"The syntax of the first line is dodgy
and the second full of clichés."
"Certainly."
"The meaning of the fourth is obscure."
"Sure."
"Axe those adjectives, they weaken the emotion".
"Interesting notion."
"The fifth line is rather pompous
but the last line is marvellous.
I should definitely keep that line!"
"Ah fine!"
……………………

"Next."

(I knew they'd love it.)

There is No Escaping Poets

It was in the year two thousand and ten
and as Nostradamus predicted
a plague got hold of our nation.
In every corner of every street
someone was possessed of fever for declamation.

Alas no-one was safe from poets!

Allegories, alliterations, metaphors galore,
clichés, puns, similes willy-nilly,
blank verse, free verse, verse everywhere,
slant rhyme, internal rhyme, assonance,
tetrameter, trimeter, tribach, trochee, consonance

held no secrets for poets!

But the mere sound of a rhyme
sent the non-convert to crime.
Someone tried to shoot all the poets
but soon ran out of ammunition.
Others try to gag or strangle them
but before expiring, in their last breath
managed to utter a Shakespearian sonnet.
Indeed it was an impossible task
to get rid of (bloody) poets!

Although the judge pitied verse-haters
(having himself a poetry-spouting spouse)
he had to have them put away.
They were not sad to go to Reading jail,
Borstal or Holloway.
With jubilation they sang:

"No more tercets, triolets, quatrains, cinquains, sestets,
no more pantoums, rubaits or sonnets,
no more limericks, rondeaux, rondels,
out with kyrielles, ballads and villanelles!"
But as the door creaked to shut, the villains' hearts
sank in hearing the voice of the poet in residence claim
"Here rehabilitation starts with a poem!"

Poets Come to Us

And you will be received with open arms and a cup of tea.
We welcome everyone in our midst
- all genders – even the heterosexual minority
and all nationalities (French can restrain, we have already one too many.)
If to rhyme or not to rhyme is your question, do not to worry, rhyming is not mandatory and generally not recommended.
If you don't know your Clerihew from your Haiku
or your Gazal from your Tanga
there is a chance no one else will have a clue.
We will help you relentlessly and with much patience.
If we can't make sense of the poem
you have painfully penned, a nice soul will find one
and you will be surprised at the deep meaning
you didn't know was there (nor did anyone else).
Yes, come dear poet and join us.
You will be rewarded with greater knowledge
and a cup of tea.

Cost: Four Pounds

From a Poet to Another

Your poem is music
-melodies that shred the air,
a flutter in the breeze.
It is a painting
-droplets of blue distilling a landscape
with fluid brush strokes.
It is a dance
-a flight to the Gods
in Nijinsky's arms.

Your poem refreshes,
like a stream in a mountain,
like an oasis in the desert.
It's a gift of a smile, a thought, a tear,
a blaze.

All Change

For decades I have tried to emulate the Engleesh
and I believe that I have largely succeeded
in reaching the summit of Englishness:
my upper lip is so stiff it could hold a plate.
If I see a queue I am sure to join it.
My wit and self-deprecation are second to none.
Any sign of crisis and I rush to make a cup of tea.
My vocabulary on the subject of weather is unsurpassed.

Were those efforts in vain?

Now the nation is undergoing a mutation:
their upper lip quivers and collapses,
emotions run high and eyes fill up at the least upset.
Kissing supplants the firm handshake and
It is with *effroi* that I see that their famous *sang-froid* is a
vanishing trait. They now drink gallons of capucinni
instead of that soothing cup of tea.
I was so relieved when the other day my friend exclaimed,
"Unusual weather for this time of the year, don't you
think?!"

To Be or Not to Be

To be or not to be? ponders the Prince of Denmark.
If only he knew of Descartes's remark:
“I think therefore I am.” Many a student of language
would have been delighted by the lack of verbiage.
But lovers 'de la comedia del Arte'
and admirers of Shakespearian sonnets
would be *désolés* by the brevity of that soliloquy.
Not to mention the frustration of actors wanting
to demonstrate the brilliance of their performance
in such a short sentence.
What if Descartes took the decision
to invert that proposition?
“I am therefore I think.” Well, that is really a question!

Balinese walk

At Dempasar
dampness envelopes
spreading lassitude.

Kuta roars
motorbikes and sea.
Tourists are preyed upon.

Up on the hill
silence and solitude
caress the soul.

A cassia sheds blossoms,
droplets of blood
staining arid soil.

Black on white
dead branches sprout plumes,
egrets pausing.

Dotted on the island
baskets overflowing...
offerings placating gods.

The sun is an orange
gobbled up by the sea.
Diving I find empty waters.
the moon smiles thinly at my foolishness.

Fishing boats in the night,
Fireflies dancing on the waves.
Will the gods help the catch?

Dawn downcast
fishermen's nets are empty.
Will the gods be kinder tomorrow?

Fish,
rainbows darting
in and out the coral reef.

Under the Banyan trees
in a tangle of limbs young boys dream.
On coffee skin, opals glisten...

Before the sacred ceremony
men and women bathe.
Gods like their adorers clean.

Villagers are in sarongs embroidered
for fairytale princes and princesses.
At midnight the feast will be over.

Now they make their way
through lush rice fields
carrying gifts on their heads.

On entering the temple
music enslaves our ears,
Bells bewitching...

Bejewelled girls
weave a dance around the temple.
Gods smile at their grace.

In cumbersome bodies we watch
sweat bursting on our white skin.
We are out of place.

Fruits impaled into pyramids,
suckling pigs crackle.
The gods are greedy.

Villagers snake their way home.
Tonight they'll go hungry,
But the gods are sated.

Parrots squawk, monkeys chatter,
the jungle luxuriates.
A rainstorm shows the gods' gratitude.

Rejoice...The pyre is alight,
ashes scattered.
Ancestors will be reborn.

Don't Be Too Hard on the Greeks

They made our civilisation.
Philosophers, scientists, poets, mathematicians,
(imagine all the problems sans Pythagoras's theorem),
builders extraordinaire and musicians
graced that ancient nation.

Yes, be lenient on that race
if they echo their gods frolicking on Mount Olympus,
and rather play with Venus than count on the abacus.
There, the epicurean way is commonplace.
(To save on the washing up they break the plates.)

Please don't make a drama out of the Drachma.
Be heroic: help vestals to rekindle the flame
and find the thread into the labyrinth to either tame
or slay the monster with twenty-seven tentacles.

Defy Delphi's oracle which predicts
the demise of that nation. Yes, be stoic
and for Zeus's sake stick up for the gamely Greek.

Prague

And now tourists gasp
at its facades of Tuscany rose,
Prussian blue and Viennese cream,
behind which leap, spiralled
black towers of Gothic castles
haunted by forgotten vampires.

Princes, musicians, paupers, soldiers
have danced, sung, begged and died
on Prague's perfect stage.

And now a gypsy with weary eyes
plays an eerie tune on Bohemian glass,
while over the Vltava
the bridge is crowded with strangers
masquerading as friends,
spreading like weeds,
invading, strangling, suffocating
your flowering city.

On Prague's perfect stage
princes, musicians, paupers, soldiers
lived, danced, sang, begged and died.

Gypsy Days

I left my footprints
on the cool stones of the old town
- Gypsy days in Dubrovnik -

The echo of my guitar and the voices
of Bebbo, Luca, Sophia and Mikhael
still haunt the air, in Dubrovnik.

We sang Beatles songs
to celebrate freedom
in Dubrovnik.

We were Beatniks,
high on love and Slivovich
in Dubrovnik.

I saw no shadows
as we waved goodbye to those friends
from Dubrovnik.

But as our battered car
stumbled along the lonely coast
I felt my throat tightening

and was silenced by the eeriness
of the blackening mountains
and the reddening sea.

For a moment a ripple of uncertainty
disturbed my insouciance as we sped away
from Dubrovnik.

Stalking Flowers

In early spring chill I pick snowdrops,
'February virgins' shivering,
in silver goblets, they please my eyes.

Alas time that fades and bruises
robs me of their dazzle.

In mid-spring sun I gather daffodils.
Gangling stems snap under my fingers.
Brash adolescents in crystal vases, they please my eyes.

Time dulls the waxy shine,
disintegrates stalks in cloudy water.

In summers' enchanted gardens, I steal roses,
cradling in my arms, thorns deep in my flesh.
Scent fills the room...I drift back into the past:
Mother's dress is the velvet of roses and …

in autumn wind I wander into woods and fields,
collecting branches heavy with berries.
In baskets of straw they please my eyes.

Once more time mutilates, spills juices
staining the dark polish floor.

Enraged I run into the frozen air.
Winter has laid a shroud.
No more life – nothing more.
Bereft I leave for the city.

Sweet flowers, prisoners of time,
sorcerer whose brutal touch
transforms all beauty, leaving decay.

Déjeuner sur L'Herbe

Fields were ballrooms
where I danced with poppies and cornflowers.

Rivers fizzed white waters
and flashed silver fish. I, lost mermaid,
splashed and dived in their opalescent trail.

With swifts I flew and whizzed around houses
inviting people to romp in the azure.

To pause
I slipped into a painting and with courtesans,
I reclined under a luscious tree, watching the passers-by
gaze at our captured perfection.

Heat intoxicated and dazed my senses
making dream and reality tangible.

That summer all was possible.

My Grave, My Cradle

The sea's incessant caress made me a sunken city.*
Once I stretched to skies,
now glacial darkness engulfs my walls.
Where jasmine and pomegranate grew
seaweeds fan and swoon.
Fading mosaics and crumbling colonnades
are vestiges of my past.
Come, stranger, though your eyes, let us relive my life:

Dawn brings silvered nets, treasures for the market.
Traders shout. Fruits, spices, sour and sweet, brocades and
silks to drape on sinuous sirens.
Chariots' wheels stun the cobbled streets.
Aphrodite's temple gathers worshippers. Whisperers...
At the zenith, life ebbs a-while.

Long shadows bring a roaring crowd;
gladiators are poised to pounce.
At dusk, the tide steals boats away.

Rocking of waves will further my destruction until,
dust tossed on shores, I might rise to be a new city.

* The sunken city is Simena, off the shores of Kekova in Turkey

Summer Song

For a moment the crickets
cease their racket.
In the torpor of the afternoon
we can hear the idle steps of a tourist,
a diver's splash cooling the air
and the *froufrou* of sycamore leaves
that the breeze caresses.
Soon the crickets resume their serenade.

Chanson d'Été

Brièvement les cigales suspendent leur chant
et dans la torpeur de midi on peut entendre
les pas nonchalants d'un promeneur,
un plongeon mouillé qui rafraîchit l'atmosphère
et le froissement de feuilles de sycomore
que la brise caresse.
Mais bientôt les cigales reprennent leur sérénade
envoûtante.

The Cuckoo to the Nightingale

"Your plumage is dull!" said cuckoo to nightingale.
"It's true," replied the nightingale,
"Your feathers might be brighter than mine
but when I herald spring, roses open.
Your two notes coucou, a pathetic effort
which cannot be compared with my arpeggios!
At night I sing alone and lovers sigh."

"Well, I am sure it's all lovely,
stay in your garden, charm your lovers,
while I travel the world and fly hither
and thither to discover new shores.
What do you say to that?"

"I care not about your prowess.
You are a villain! Squatting and stealing.
Moreover, your name is attached to ridicule
while mine is linked to a tragic legend of sacrifice.
In the name of love, would you like to hear it?"

"No time, I am off."
"Coucou," Cuckoo added.

Intruder

a smell of cabbage soup and other
indefinable odours lie in lumps

bits of food and mess
the enraged cat flies around the kitchen

the grandfather's grimacing head
floats in clouds of smoke

on the table empty bottles
and a glass half full the liquid
matching the father's nose

the tattooed mother is lost in a puzzle
upstairs a baby cries

I said *you must feed him and change him*
at regular intervals

sure says the mother
dazed by the blue
sky she has just created

Puzzle

Don't look now
the picture is incomplete
a piece of blue sky is missing.

A river flows,
spring blossoms on trees.
On grassy banks
lovers are kissing,

but a piece of sky is missing.

For you my child,
I wanted a perfect world
but there is a gap I cannot fill
someone has lost that bit of sky.

Fallen

Ivy encircles your waist.
A crown of convolvulus interlaces with hair
that snakes between Verdigris breasts
then sweeps down a crumbling pedestal.
Swathed in a netting of cobweb,
only your smile intact,
you lie on a bed of nettles
forgotten.

Splinters of light reveal your secret:
under that pitted crust of lichen
you are made of marble...
Newly carved and unaware of destiny, you smiled.
Dazzling amongst mortals,
You once stood in golden rooms,
admired, desired.

Reflections

It was a bird's wing,
a light touch that sent us spinning.
It was the autumn sun,
brilliance without warmth.

Another came,
You turned away.
The mirage held in each other's eyes vanished
as a ripple disturbs a reflection.

Broken Love

Silk is made of your hair,
gold is made from your heart,
clouds are made in your mind,
broken glass made to wound me.
And the clock beats the little time
left to love you.

Love you as softly as silk,
love you as some treasure gold,
love you as lightly as clouds,
without broken glass to wound me.
Please ask the clock to stop time.

Blue is my Colour

Blue is what I see
when my lover wakes me,
his eyes watching over me, over me.

Blue is what I feel
when my lover leaves me,
longing, longing.

Blue is what we do
when he returns,
eagerly, so eagerly.

Midnight blue
holds the secret
of what we do, of what we do!

Language of Fans

The room *frissonne*
as a cascade of ostrich plumes
or point de Gaze lace
cools the air.

She holds *une fête champêtre*:
Villagers dancing in fields,
flowers and butterflies *pêle-mêle.*
When he sees her,
la belle magicienne folds the landscape,
robbing us of birds in summer sky.

She rests her fan against her heart: I belong to you.
Touching her mouth: Don't betray our secret.
Caressing the ivory ribs and
unfurling the leaves: I long to see you later.
The gallant acquiesces,
they will meet under the stars.

She sighs as she anticipates,
his hands unlacing her bodice
and untying her crinoline
that encircles her waist like a cage.

Unaware of her agitation,
the ballroom swings and *pirouette.*
Furtive glances glide
to capture messages borne
on the trembling wings of fans.

Hollywood Boobs

You may drool
at those boobs
that don't move
that don't droop
that don't feel.

But don't fool
with those boobs,
as pressure endangers
and punctures could occur.
Conclusion -
Explosion!

No more boobs
that don't move
that don't droop
that don't feel.

♪♫Boo – Boo – De - Boo♪♫

Sacrifice

We are drowning in oceans of chocolate,
midnight blue and burgundy velvets,
mint, cream and peach satin,
cascades of jet, amber and gold necklaces.

What should we buy?
Whispering silks to entice lovers,
plunging necklines to tempt others
or a diaphanous negligee?

Now we sip tea
comparing our hoards to enslave,
exclaiming at the price of things,
blaming the models' rewards.
What of those children in sweatshops?
They should be banned.
What would be the alternative? Prostitution?

A silence falls...

“I think I shall buy those high-heeled mules.”
“And I, the set of divine underwear.”

Outside the cold bounced off our furs.
Roasted chestnuts filled us with memories
of our magic childhood.
The stars winked at us
pleased at our good deed.

The Woods Declare Love to the Foxgloves

For too long darkness has haunted my lair!
in deep slumber dreams of you held away despair.
Fleeting visitors have gone,
ephemeral distractions.
I long for you.
Please, please come, come to me.

Days stretch and bloom
weaving me a coat of velveteen
inviting you to unfurl swatches
of blue, pink and mauve satin.
At last summer guests
you've come to me.

Open your corollas
lascivious belles, swaying
to the rhythm of a bird's orchestra.
Reticent guests,
stay, stay with me.

I'll be your vessel, your guardian, your lover
until September sprays my robe a golden rust
and crinkles your skirt,
until October, November fade my brocade
and turn you into clouds on stilts
drifting to the corners of my solitude,
so next year in multitudes
you'll come back to me.

Pity the Poor Embryo

Mother don't worry.
You want a blue-eyed baby?
Take a little cell here
add another one there
and hey presto
you'll have a perfect embryo!

Alas Cyrano would never have made that prose
about his nose
if they'd taken a little cell here
added another there
to have a perfect embryo.

As for Napoleon, Nero
and other dubious heroes,
they'd never have had to fight
to prove their height.
They wouldn't have been so nasty
for posterity.
Because with a little cell here
and a little cell there
they would have been perfect.

Someone previously
had a similar idea,
but could not wait
for that magic potion.
and found a radical solution
to rid his nation
of all its imperfections.

Apocalypse

A cherub has lost bow and arrow
and the angel his wings and halo
the bronze figure of a fisherman *sans* rod
has caught a fish.
Marilyn's bust is chipped.
Snow White sits on a one-legged stool,
only five and half dwarves are present,
a guitar without strings hangs
beside an empty canvas,
the lead soldiers' rifles are missing.
Mary has lost Jesus and God his head.
Only a stone statue of a goblin is intact.
With malevolent glare, he reigns supreme,
over this poor, poor broken world.

For the Earth

Our life on hold, the earth breathes.

The curtain of pollution lifts
and skies dazzle.
On the dark velvet robe of night
jewels sparkle
and from afar a child sees a star
for the very first time.

Life on hold, the earth breathes.

Cities are deserted,
the heaving mass of people has vanished.
Ships have ceased from pouring filth.
In seas, canals and rivers
fish frolic in transparent waters.
Only the scent of flowers perfumes the air.
The roar of planes has died away
leaving birds' songs to enchant our day.

A malevolent magician has cursed mankind
-serendipity for the earth which breathes
while our life is on hold.

Beyond Darkness...

When trees, stripped of their ornaments stand,
black giants lost in dusk and mist, drawn
like a widow's veil to grieve and mourn,
when birds' songs have ceased and
their wings no longer beat the air,
when all creatures hide in despair,
when woods are deserted and I walk alone,
my steps crushing leaves into soil,
I wonder. Have trees always known
spring will give back their emeralds?
Does Earth know, though wrapped in voile
sun will magic life with a sprinkle of golds?
And do we know when our heart has frozen with tears,
love will bring hope and dissipate all fears?

Those were the days my friend...

Do you remember those long, long summer days
and our haste to be part of the adult world?
And when the spring's palette painted rainbows in the sky
do you remember the bird song waking in our hearts
such strange feelings?
But now that autumn has chased us
into the raw bite of winter
don't you long for those interminable summer days?

Let's Party!

A few people are gathered
-a rigid and pallid-looking lot
in their starched clothing.
The music isn't exactly swinging!
And flowers look very stiff.
What is this all about? Upon my soul
it's a surprise party for me!
I am feted, praised in glorious terms.
I am in heaven.
To thank these good friends and bid them goodbye
I stand on the threshold but I am spirited away.
(What a swell parting that was.)

www.ingramcontent.com/pod-product-compliance
Ingram Content Group UK Ltd.
Pitfield, Milton Keynes, MK11 3LW, UK
UKHW042000190726
13854UKWH00005B/2076

9 781800 314177